What Is the Best Pet?

by Mrs. Ewing's and Ms. Nance's classes
with Tony Stead

capstone
classroom

Kittens Are the Best

by Grace and Jayshri

I think a kitten is the best pet.

3

One reason is because kittens
are cute and soft.

Another reason is because kittens like to play.

A kitten would be a great pet!

Fish Are the Best

by Daxing

I would love a fish for a pet.

A fish would be good because it can swim!

A fish would also make a good
pet because it does not bark!

Would you rather have a kitten or a fish?